Special Order Recipes
Low Fat, Low Carb, High Protein
Over 120 Variations on 25 of my favorite recipes

by

Janice O'Bryan

⚜

On the front cover (Oat Bran White Pizza-page 18, Chipotle Pork Tenderloin-page 50, and Lemon Garlic Shrimp-page 35)

Editor: Nicole Thomson

Recipes and Photos: Janice O'Bryan
Cover: Nicole Thomson

First Edition. Printed in the United States of America

ISBN: 1463765622
ISBN-13: 978-1463765620

See Your Doctor First

This recipe book is designed to provide helpful information on the subjects addressed. This book is sold with the understanding that the author is not rendering medical, or health advice, or any other personal services. Please consult your personal physician before commencing any diet or exercise regime. You should rely on your physician's advice regarding whether any diet is appropriate for you, and to establish your weight goal. The author disclaims all liability associated with the recommendations and guidelines set forth in this book.

❧

<u>Acknowledgments</u>

Thanks to Tom who loves everything I cook, good or bad, just because I made it.

Thanks to my family and friends who have fully supported my "hobby" for all these years.

And special thanks to Nicole for all the technical support and friendship she has given me!

⚜

Our motto at Special Order Recipes...

"Substitutions are not only welcomed, but expected!"

Notes From The Author

This is a collection of recipes dedicated to keeping refined sugar, high fat and simple-carbohydrate ingredients out while keeping natural sweeteners, high protein and complex-carbohydrates in. Keeping food low in fat means cutting out the oils we use in our daily regime. Keeping refined sugars and processed white flour out of our diets means keeping the food low in simple-carbohydrates. Including foods in our diet like bran and whole grains means adding heart-healthy, complex-carbohydrates.

Who actually goes a restaurant and orders straight from the menu these days? More often than not there is one thing you want added, or removed from the dish. Sometimes both! How often is an order placed with 'hold the cheese', 'sauce on the side' 'no rice but double the vegetables? We do not let these few ingredients make us order something else. I will prove to you that the days are gone when we should prepare food just by reading a recipe. Cooking has evolved to such a level that any recipe can be adapted to a persons' likes and/or dietary needs. I will teach you how to de-mystify the personalization of a recipe; I will challenge you to customize the recipe to fit your own tastes.

That is the basic principle behind Special Order Recipes. Substituting, adding and changing recipe ingredients to make it **your** dish.

Every section in this book begins with a BASIC RECIPE. This is the most broken down, simple version of the recipe: the foundation. From there you build something new each time... but you always START with the BASIC RECIPE and just continue to add. You will learn them easily and with the variations I provide in this book, you will see the endless possibilities with simple additions or substitutions. Many of the recipes can be divided and made into 2 or 3 different versions so never again will anyone have to say there's nothing new to make for dinner!

In March 2011, Nicole and I set out on the Dukan Diet, a diet that focuses on foods low in fat and carbohydrates and high in protein. We decided to create DukanItOut.com: a website full of recipes that people could make easily and follow these simple guide-lines. It would be a great way to have fun, while helping others stick with the diet. We successfully reached our goal weights on time and continued blogging and posting recipes on the website. This book includes a lot of our favorite recipes from the site, plus many new ones.

Enjoy!
Janice

Eggs

BASIC EGG RECIPE

2 cups egg white substitute (or 8 eggs)
1/4 cup fat free milk

Whisk the eggs and milk together. Season with salt and pepper.

Serves 4

SMOKED SALMON AND DILL SCRAMBLE
BASIC EGG RECIPE
2 green onions, thinly sliced
6 oz smoked salmon, cut into strips
1 T fresh dill, chopped
1/2 cup fat free cream cheese

1. Spray a warmed non-stick skillet with cooking spray. Add the onions and sauté for 2 minutes. Add the egg mixture and cook on low heat for about 5 minutes, adding the salmon and dill in the last minute.
2. Remove from heat and dot eggs with cream cheese.

FILET MIGNON SCRAMBLE
BASIC EGG RECIPE
1 8 oz filet mignon
1/4 cup chives, chopped
1/2 cup fat free sour cream

1. Cook the filet in a sauté pan for 5 minutes on each side. Set aside to cool and slice.
2. Add the egg mixture and cook on low heat for about 5 minutes, adding the meat in the last minute.
3. Serve with chives and sour cream.

Eggs

SPINACH AND MUSHROOM QUICHE
BASIC EGG RECIPE

1 8 oz package sliced mushrooms
2 cups baby spinach leaves
a pinch of freshly grated nutmeg
3/4 cup Gruyere cheese, grated or any fat free
shredded cheese
2 T Parmesan cheese, grated

1. Add the mushrooms to a skillet and sauté in a bit of cooking spray until brown. Add the spinach and nutmeg and cook until wilted.
2. Spray a 9-inch glass pie pan with cooking spray and pour the egg mixture in. Sprinkle vegetables and cheeses over the eggs and push down with the back of a spoon.
3. Bake at 350 until the quiche is just set in the center, about 40-45 minutes.

MEATBALL FRITTATA
BASIC EGG RECIPE

1/2 small onion, chopped
1 package Tofu Shirataki angel hair noodles,
chopped into 4-inch pieces
6-8 leftover meatballs (pages 9-13), roughly chopped
2 T Parmesan cheese, finely grated

1. Add the onions to a skillet and sauté in a bit of cooking spray until soft.
2. Spray a 9-inch glass pie pan with cooking spray and pour the egg mixture in. Sprinkle noodles, meatballs, onions, and cheese over the eggs and push down with the back of a spoon.
3. Bake at 350 until the eggs are just set in the center, about 40-45 minutes.

Eggs

MEXICAN SCRAMBLE
BASIC EGG RECIPE
1 serrano chili, finely chopped (seeds removed if you don't like the fire!)
2 T red onions, finely chopped
2 T red bell pepper, finely chopped
1 small tomato, chopped
2 T cilantro, chopped
2 T fat free sour cream

1. Spray a warmed non-stick skillet with cooking spray. Add the vegetables and sauté until soft, about 5 minutes.
2. Add the egg mixture and cook on low heat for about 5 minutes.

VEGGIE EGG SCRAMBLE
BASIC EGG RECIPE
1 small onion, thinly sliced
1/2 red bell pepper, thinly sliced
4 mushrooms, thinly sliced
4 stalks asparagus, chopped into 1-inch pieces
1 cup packed spinach

1. Spray a warmed non-stick skillet with cooking spray. Add the vegetables and sauté until soft, about 5 minutes.
2. Add the egg mixture and cook on low heat for about 5 minutes.

ITALIAN SCRAMBLE
BASIC EGG RECIPE
1/2 red bell pepper, chopped or sliced
1 shallot, finely chopped
1 small plum tomato, seeded and chopped
2 T chopped parsley
1 T chopped basil
1 T leftover pizza sauce (page 18)
1 T shredded Parmesan cheese

1. Spray a warmed non-stick skillet with olive oil spray. Add the bell pepper and shallot, cook for a minute and pour in the eggs.
2. Once the bottom has set, start to stir the eggs and when they are almost fully cooked, add the tomato and continue to cook for one more minute.
3. Garnish with parsley, basil, warmed pizza sauce and Parmesan.

Eggs

EGGS WITH RATATOUILLE
BASIC EGG RECIPE
2 plum tomatoes, chopped
1/2 small onion, chopped
4 cloves garlic, minced
1/2 small red bell pepper, chopped
1/2 small yellow bell pepper, chopped
1/2 large eggplant, cubed
5 large mushrooms, roughly chopped
1 medium zucchini, quartered and sliced
1 T fresh parsley, chopped
1/4 cup basil leaves, torn
1/4 t red pepper flakes
1 t balsamic vinegar

1. Sauté the first 6 ingredients in a bit of cooking spray. Cover and simmer until vegetables are soft, about 20 minutes.
2. Add the mushrooms and zucchini, parsley and basil and season with salt and peppers. Add the vinegar, cover and cook for another 15 minutes. If the vegetables dry out, add a bit of water until they are soft.
3. Serve over scrambled eggs or form into a plain omelet.

4

Salads

BASIC CHOPPED SALAD RECIPE

1 head iceberg lettuce, chopped
1 small cucumber, quartered, seeded and sliced
3 plum tomatoes, quartered, seeded and chopped

Toss all ingredients together and drizzle with
vinaigrette.

Serves 2 as an entrée or 4 as an appetizer

BASIC VINAIGRETTE RECIPE

1 small shallot, finely chopped
3 T balsamic, red or white wine vinegar
1 t olive oil or 2 T water

Let shallot marinate in the vinegar for 5 minutes.
Slowly whisk in the olive oil. Season with salt and
pepper.

CAPRESE CHOPPED SALAD
BASIC CHOPPED SALAD RECIPE
3 oz goat cheese
1/4 cup sun-dried tomatoes, chopped
1/2 cup packed basil leaves, torn

Serve with Caesar Vinaigrette and Garlic Parmesan
Flatbread (page 8)

CAESAR VINAIGRETTE
BASIC VINAIGRETTE RECIPE
reduce vinegar to 2 T and add 2 T lemon juice
1 T Dijon mustard
1 large garlic clove, crushed

Mix well and keep in an airtight jar.

Salads

SALADE NICOISE
BASIC CHOPPED SALAD RECIPE
1/2 lb green beans, blanched and cut into 2-inch pieces
1 can of tuna in water, flaked or fresh sushi-grade tuna
3 hard-boiled eggs, quartered
1 T shallots, finely chopped
1-2 T capers
3-4 anchovy fillets
a handful of nicoise olives
1/2 cup sweet grape tomatoes, halved
1/2 t fresh thyme, chopped
1/2 t fresh tarragon, chopped

Serve with Herbs de Provence Vinaigrette

HERBS DE PROVENCE VINAIGRETTE
BASIC VINAIGRETTE RECIPE
2 t Herbs de Provence
or you can make your own for future use:

Herbs de Provence
3 T dried marjoram
3 T dried thyme
3 T dried savory
2 t lavender flowers
1 t dried basil
1 t dried rosemary
1/2 t fennel seeds

Mix well and keep in an airtight jar.

CREAMY ICEBERG AND CHERRY TOMATO SLAW
BASIC CHOPPED SALAD RECIPE
3 T low fat buttermilk
3 T plain Greek yogurt
1 T parsley, chopped
1 T shallot or sweet onion, finely chopped

Mix all the ingredients and refrigerate until you are ready to serve. Top with freshly ground pepper.

6

Salads

ITALIAN CHOPPED SALAD
BASIC CHOPPED SALAD RECIPE
1/2 cup roasted peppers, chopped
1/2 cup fat free mozzarella, cubed
2 carrots, blanched and chopped
1/4 lb green beans, blanched, cut into 1-inch pieces
1/4 cup low fat salami, cubed
1/4 cup turkey pepperoni, sliced into thin strips

Serve with Basic Balsamic Vinaigrette (page 5)

SOUTHWEST CHICKEN CHOPPED SALAD
BASIC CHOPPED SALAD RECIPE
1/2 cup cooked chicken breast, cubed
2 T Real Bacon Bits
1/4 cup fat free cheddar cheese, cubed
1/4 cup jicama, cubed
1 roasted Anaheim chili, seeded and sliced
1/2 cup cilantro, chopped

Serve with Chipotle Ranch Creamy Vinaigrette and Jalapeno Flatbread

CHIPOTLE RANCH CREAMY VINAIGRETTE
BASIC VINAIGRETTE RECIPE
1 t adobo sauce from the canned chipotle chilis
2 T fat free sour cream
1/4 t lemon juice
1/2 t dried parsley
1/4 t onion powder
1/4 t garlic powder
1 chive, finely chopped
a pinch of dry mustard
a pinch of paprika

Mix well and keep in an airtight jar.

Flatbreads

BASIC OAT BRAN FLATBREAD RECIPE

1 packet of rapid rise active yeast
1/4 cup warm water
1/4 cup of oat bran
a pinch of salt
1/2 t olive oil

Instructions:
1. Pour yeast over the warm water and let it sit for 10 minutes until it starts to bubble.
2. Place the bowl over simmering water and add the oat bran, a pinch of salt, olive oil, and any addition. Stir constantly, until a very sticky ball of dough forms. Keep stirring until the moisture is absorbed and it resembles a ball of dough.
3. Spray a glass bowl with olive oil spray; place the dough in the bowl, cover with a kitchen towel and let rise in a warm place for an hour. The dough will not rise much but it will lose its stickiness and become much easier to handle.
4. Place pizza stone in the oven and preheat to 425. Place the dough between two pieces of parchment paper and roll it out until it's cracker-thin (should be about a 7-inch circle). Cut the dough into 2-inch wide strips. Spray both sides with olive oil spray, place the strips on a new piece of parchment paper, and place on the pre-warmed pizza stone.
5. If using cheese, shred with a fine microplane to just get a bit of cheese over the top of the pieces. Season with salt and pepper and bake at 425 for 12 minutes.

Makes 2 servings

GARLIC PARMESAN FLATBREAD
BASIC OAT BRAN FLATBREAD RECIPE
1 t Parmesan cheese, finely shredded
1 garlic clove, crushed

JALAPENO FLATBREAD
BASIC OAT BRAN FLATBREAD RECIPE
1 t jalapeno, finely chopped
1 t smoked Gouda, finely shredded

CHEDDAR AND BACON FLATBREAD
BASIC OAT BRAN FLATBREAD RECIPE
1 t Real Bacon Bits
1 t cheddar, finely shredded

DRIED BLUEBERRY LEMON FLATBREAD
BASIC OAT BRAN FLATBREAD RECIPE
1 t Splenda® or 1/2 T Brown Sugar Blend Splenda®
or 1 T honey
1 t lemon zest
1 T dried blueberries
1/4 t cinnamon

8

Meatballs

BASIC MEATBALL RECIPE

1 lb ground meat
1/4 cup egg white substitute or 1 egg
4 T oat bran
1/2 small onion, finely chopped
salt and black pepper or red pepper flakes

Mix all ingredients by hand, careful not to handle it too much.

Bake Instructions: Preheat oven to 400. On a baking sheet bake smaller meatballs for 15 minutes, larger meatballs for 22-25 minutes. If serving with sauce, add meatballs to sauce and heat together in a saucepan.

Brown and Sauté Instructions: Sauté meatballs in a skillet on medium heat until brown. Add 1/4 cup water to the skillet, cover, and steam for another 3-5 minutes, or until fully cooked.

Serves 4 as an entrée or 6 as an appetizer.

9

SWEET AND SOUR CHICKEN MEATBALLS
BASIC MEATBALL RECIPE
1 lb ground chicken breast
1/2 t onion powder
1/2 t garlic powder

Form 15 2-inch meatballs-See Bake Instructions-Serve with Sweet and Sour Sauce

Sweet and Sour Sauce
12 oz tomato sauce
1 1/2 cups water
1/2 cup Brown Sugar Blend Splenda® or 1/4 cup Splenda®
1/4 cup lemon juice
1/2 t red pepper flakes

Simmer all ingredients in a saucepan for 15 minutes.

Meatballs

2. Add the rest of the ingredients and cook for 15 minutes. Season with salt and pepper.
3. Using a hand blender or food processor, process until it's a chunky sauce.

CUMIN-INFUSED TURKEY MEATBALLS WITH SPICY EGGPLANT SAUCE
BASIC MEATBALL RECIPE
1 lb ground turkey
3 garlic cloves, finely chopped
1/2 t cumin
a pinch of ground cinnamon

Form 20 meatballs-See Bake Instructions-Serve with Sweet and Spicy Cumin Eggplant Sauce

Sweet and Spicy Cumin Eggplant Sauce
1/2 large eggplant, small cubed
1/2 small onion, finely chopped
3 cloves of garlic, finely minced
1 T Brown Sugar Blend Splenda®
1 T cider vinegar
14 oz can fire-roasted tomatoes
8 oz beef stock
2 T ancho chili powder
1 T smoked hot paprika
2 T dried parsley

1. Sauté eggplant, onion and garlic for 5 minutes in a bit of cooking spray.

MOROCCAN BEEF MEATBALLS WITH YOGURT-PARSLEY DIP
BASIC MEATBALL RECIPE
1 1/4 lbs ground sirloin
2 garlic cloves, minced
1/4 cup parsley, chopped
1/4 cup cilantro, chopped
1 t paprika
1/2 t cumin
1/2 t cayenne pepper

Form 30 mini meatballs-See Bake Instructions-Serve with Yogurt-Parsley Dip

Yogurt-Parsley Dip
6 oz fat free plain Greek yogurt
1/4 cup parsley, chopped
1 t lemon zest

Mix all ingredients and season with salt and pepper.

Meatballs

PEPPERONI PIZZA MEATBALLS
BASIC MEATBALL RECIPE
1/2 lb ground turkey Italian sausage
1/2 lb ground beef
1 T tomato paste
3 garlic cloves, finely chopped
1/4 cup turkey pepperoni, chopped
2 oz mozzarella, cubed
2 T Italian parsley, chopped

Form 20 meatballs-See Bake Instructions

These are delicious served with Basic Pasta Sauce (page 24)

MEATBALLS WITH CHIPOTLE PLUM SAUCE
BASIC MEATBALL RECIPE
1/2 lb ground pork
1/2 lb ground beef
3 garlic cloves, finely chopped
1/2 cup raisins
1/4 cup cilantro, chopped

Form 20 meatballs-See Bake Instructions-Serve with Chipotle Plum Sauce

Chipotle Plum Sauce
1/2 small onion, finely chopped
15 oz can tomato sauce
2 ripe plums, chopped
2 T adobo sauce
1 chipotle chili, chopped

Sauté onion in a bit of cooking spray. Add the rest of the ingredients and simmer for 15 minutes.

Meatballs

STICKY TURKEY MEATBALLS
BASIC MEATBALL RECIPE
1 1/4 lb ground turkey meat
1 t garlic salt
1/2 t dried ginger
1 t smoked Paprika
1/2-1 t red pepper flakes

Form 15 2-inch meatballs-See Bake Instructions-
Serve with Sticky Sauce.

Sticky Sauce
4 t Splenda® or 1/3 cup Brown Sugar Splenda®
1/2 cup water
1 T Worcestershire sauce
1/2 t red pepper flakes
1/4 cup soy sauce
1 T cornstarch mixed with 1 T water

1. Whisk together sweetener, water, Worcestershire sauce, red pepper flakes and soy sauce until well blended and pour over meatballs. Continue to cook for an additional 15 minutes.
2. Turn down to medium heat and add the cornstarch mixture to the sauce. Cook for 2-3 minutes until sauce thickens. Serve meatballs with the sauce.

SWEDISH MEATBALLS
BASIC MEATBALL RECIPE
1 lb ground chicken
1/4 t ground nutmeg
1/4 cup egg white substitute

Form 20 meatballs-See Brown and Sauté Instructions-Serve with Mushroom Sauce

Mushroom Sauce
1 8 oz package baby portobello mushrooms, quartered
1 cup low sodium chicken broth
1 T cornstarch
1 cup fat free sour cream
2 T chopped fresh parsley

1. Sauté the mushrooms and remove them from the pan.
2. Add the chicken broth and cornstarch, stirring with a whisk until combined. Bring to a boil, and cook 1 minute, stirring constantly.
3. Stir in sour cream and return the meatballs and mushrooms to pan. Cook for 10 minutes or until meatballs are done and sauce is thick. Serve with fresh parsley.

Meatballs

SHRIMP AND PORK MEATBALLS
BASIC MEATBALL RECIPE
1/2 lb extra lean ground pork
1/2 lb shrimp, deveined, peeled and chopped
3 green onions, finely chopped
4 oz water chestnuts, finely chopped
3 T cilantro, chopped
1/2 t red pepper flakes

Form 15 2-inch meatballs-See Brown and Sauté Instructions-Serve with Asian Sweet and Spicy Dipping Sauce

Asian Sweet and Spicy Dipping Sauce
1/4 cup unseasoned rice wine vinegar
1 green onion, finely chopped
1/2 t red chili paste
2 t Splenda®
1 T lime juice
1 t soy sauce

Mix ingredients together and refrigerate until ready to use.

13

WONTON SOUP
4 cups low sodium chicken broth
1/4 t chili paste
5 oz water chestnuts, sliced and halved
4 small mushrooms, quartered
1 small zucchini, cut lengthwise and sliced
2 green onions, greens cut into 2-inch pieces, whites chopped
1/2 recipe of **SHRIMP AND PORK MEATBALLS**
1/4 lb sugar snap peas or snow peas

1. Bring broth to a boil. Add all the ingredients down to the meatballs and simmer for 20 minutes.
2. Add the peas in the last 5 minutes.

Chicken Tenders and Wings

BASIC CHICKEN TENDER & WING RECIPE

1 lb chicken tenders or skinless wings

Season chicken with salt and pepper.

Bake Instructions: Bake tenders at 450 for 12 minutes. Bake wings for 40 minutes.

Rub and Grill Instructions: Prepare rub and press on tenders. Grill 3-4 minutes per side or until done.

Sauce and Sauté Instructions: Spray pan with cooking spray. Sauté tenders in sauce for 8-10 minutes if they are left whole, 5-7 minutes if they've been pounded or cut up.

Serves 4 as an entrée or 6 as an appetizer

PARMESAN WINGS
BASIC CHICKEN TENDER & WING RECIPE
1/2 cup Parmesan cheese, the kind in the can
1/2 t cracked fresh pepper
2 T oat bran
cooking spray

Shake tenders in baggie with Parmesan, pepper and oat bran. Spray again with cooking spray-See Bake Instructions.

TANDOORI TENDERS
BASIC CHICKEN TENDER & WING RECIPE
1/2 t curry powder
1/2 t red pepper flakes
1/4 t ground ginger
1/4 t smoked paprika
1/4 t cinnamon
1/4 t turmeric
2 T water

Prepare paste with two tablespoons of water-See Rub and Grill Instructions

14

Chicken Tenders and Wings

SWEET AND SPICY ASIAN TENDERS
BASIC CHICKEN TENDER & WING RECIPE

2 T low sodium soy sauce
2 t Splenda®
1/4 cup water
1 t tomato paste
1 T sherry
1 garlic clove, minced
1/2 t fresh ginger, minced
red pepper flakes to taste
1 green onion, finely chopped
1 t cornstarch mixed with 1 T water

1. Mix all the ingredients down to the cornstarch in a saucepan and cook for 10 minutes.
2. Stir in the cornstarch mixture and cook for another 2-3 minutes-See Sauce and Sauté Instructions.

CHILI/SOY WINGS
BASIC CHICKEN TENDER & WING RECIPE

2/3 cup low sodium soy sauce
1/4 cup chili-garlic paste

Mix ingredients. Marinate tenders for 30 minutes in the fridge-See Bake Instructions

Chicken Tenders and Wings

UN-FRIED FRIED CHICKEN
BASIC CHICKEN TENDER & WING RECIPE

1/4 cup honey

2 T Dijon mustard

3/4 t paprika, regular, smoked, or hot

1/8 t garlic powder

1 1/2 cups bran flakes, finely crushed

1. Mix honey, Dijon, paprika and garlic powder together well, in a bowl. Place cereal in a large resealable baggie.
2. Dip the tenders into the honey mixture and then into the baggie.
3. Place the tenders on a foil-lined baking sheet, sprayed with cooking spray.
4. Spray the tenders with cooking spray once you have them all on the sheet. See-Bake Instructions.

CREAMY CHICKEN AND BROCCOLI CURRY
BASIC CHICKEN TENDER & WING RECIPE

1 onion, chopped

1 1/2 cups chicken broth

1 1/2 cups broccoli, steamed

1/2 cup fat free sour cream

1 t cornstarch, mixed in 1/4 cup water

1 1/2 t curry powder, any that you like

See-Sauce and Sauté Instructions. Remove chicken from skillet and set aside.
1. Add onion to the skillet and a bit of olive oil spray and cook for five minutes.
2. Add broth, cornstarch slurry, curry powder and season with salt and pepper. Cook for another 5-6 minutes or until the sauce has thickened a bit.
3. Return the chicken to the skillet, add the broccoli and heat for 2-3 minutes.
4. Remove from heat and stir in the sour cream.

Chicken Tenders and Wings

LEMON CHICKEN WITH PARSLEY SAUCE
BASIC CHICKEN TENDER & WING RECIPE

1 lemon, juice and all of its zest
1 t Splenda®
1 1/2 lbs chicken tenders

Combine the Splenda®, lemon juice and zest and marinate the chicken in it for 15 minutes-See Rub and Grill Instructions-Serve with Parsley Sauce.

Parsley Sauce

2/3 cup parsley, chopped
1/2 of a shallot, chopped
1 T red wine vinegar
1 T water
2 T lemon juice

Process all ingredients until smooth. Serve over chicken.

CHICKEN TIKKA MASALA RECIPE
BASIC CHICKEN TENDER & WING RECIPE

2 cups fat free Greek yogurt, divided
1 T lemon juice
1 t cumin
1 t cinnamon
1 t cayenne pepper
1 t ancho chili powder
1 T ginger, minced
1 clove garlic, minced
1 jalapeno, seeded and finely chopped
1/2 t cumin
2 t paprika (I used smoked)
1 8 oz can tomato sauce
cilantro, chopped

1. Combine the first 7 ingredients (1 cup of the yogurt), pour over chicken, cover, and refrigerate for 1 hour-See Rub and Grill Instructions.
2. Sauté garlic and jalapeno in a bit of olive oil spray in a skillet and add cumin and paprika. Stir in tomato sauce and cook for 5 minutes. Add the remaining cup of yogurt and grilled chicken back to the pan, just to reheat, about 5 minutes. Garnish with cilantro.

Oat Bran Pizza

BASIC OAT BRAN PIZZA CRUST RECIPE

1 packet of rapid rise active yeast
1/4 cup warm water
1/4 cup of oat bran
a pinch of salt
1/2 t olive oil

Instructions:
1. Pour yeast over the warm water and let it sit for 10 minutes until it starts to bubble.
2. Place the bowl over simmering water and add the oat bran, a pinch of salt and olive oil, and stir with a wire whisk until a very sticky ball of dough forms. Keep stirring until the moisture is absorbed and it resembles a ball of dough.
3. Spray a glass bowl with olive oil spray; place the dough in the bowl, cover with a kitchen towel and let rise in a warm place for an hour. The dough will not rise much but it will lose its stickiness and become much easier to handle.
4. Place pizza stone in the oven and preheat to 425. Place the dough between two pieces of parchment paper and roll it out until it's cracker-thin (should be about a 7-inch circle). Spray both sides with olive oil spray and season with salt and pepper. Place pizza crust on a piece of parchment paper and place on the pre-heated pizza stone.
5. Bake at 425 for 5 minutes; flip and bake for another 3 minutes. Remove the crust and turn the temperature up to 450.

Makes one small pizza crust.

BASIC PIZZA SAUCE RECIPE

1/4 cup tomato paste
1/8-1/4 cup water
1/2 t oregano

Mix all ingredients together and refrigerate.

OAT BRAN WHITE PIZZA (Cover Recipe)
BASIC OAT BRAN PIZZA CRUST RECIPE

2 T low fat ricotta cheese
2 T goat cheese
1/2 cup skim milk or fat free mozzarella, shredded
2 T Parmesan cheese, finely grated
3 large basil leaves, chopped

1. Spread the ricotta and goat cheeses on the crust with the back of a spoon. Follow with mozzarella and Parmesan.
2. Bake at 450 for 7-10 minutes and sprinkle with red pepper flakes and fresh basil.

Oat Bran Pizza

SAUSAGE, SWEET BELL PEPPER, JALAPENO AND SUN-DRIED TOMATO PIZZA

BASIC OAT BRAN PIZZA CRUST RECIPE
BASIC PIZZA SAUCE RECIPE

1 link turkey Italian sausage, removed from the casing and browned
1/4 yellow bell pepper, sliced thinly and sautéed
1/2 jalapeno, seeded and thinly sliced
2 T sun-dried tomatoes
1/2 cup skim milk or fat free mozzarella, shredded
2 T Parmesan cheese, finely grated

1. Spread the sauce on the crust with the back of a spoon. Follow with sausage, bell pepper, jalapeno and sun-dried tomatoes and then mozzarella and Parmesan.
2. Bake at 450 for 7-10 minutes.

BACON AND EGG BREAKFAST PIZZA

BASIC OAT BRAN PIZZA CRUST RECIPE
2 T low fat ricotta cheese
2 slices turkey bacon, cooked well and crumbled
1/2 cup egg whites or 2 eggs, scrambled
1/4 cup low or fat free cheddar cheese
2 T Parmesan cheese, finely grated

1. Spread the ricotta cheese on the crust with the back of a spoon. Follow with bacon, eggs, cheddar and Parmesan.
2. Bake at 450 for 7-10 minutes.

Oat Bran Pizza

CHICKEN, GARLIC AND BROCCOLI PIZZA
BASIC OAT BRAN PIZZA CRUST RECIPE
2 T low fat ricotta cheese
1/2 cup rotisserie chicken breast, shredded
2 cloves of garlic, thinly sliced lengthwise
1/2 cup blanched broccoli florets
1/2 cup skim milk or fat free mozzarella, shredded
2 T Parmesan cheese, finely grated

1. Spread the ricotta cheese right on the crust with the back of a spoon. Follow with chicken, garlic and broccoli and then mozzarella and Parmesan.
2. Bake at 450 for 7-10 minutes. Sprinkle with red pepper flakes.

PERFECT MUSHROOM PIZZA
BASIC OAT BRAN PIZZA CRUST RECIPE
BASIC PIZZA SAUCE RECIPE

1 8 oz package mushrooms, sliced
2 T low fat ricotta cheese
1/4 cup low or fat free mozzarella cheese
2 T Parmesan cheese, finely grated

1. Sauté the mushrooms in a bit of cooking spray careful not to stir them too much until they get a nice golden brown on one side. Flip and brown the other side. Remove from pan and season with salt and pepper.
2. Spread the sauce on the crust with the back of a spoon. Follow with mushrooms and cheeses.
3. Bake at 450 for 7-10 minutes.

Stuffed Burgers

SUN-DRIED TOMATO AND GOAT CHEESE BURGERS
BASIC STUFFED BURGER RECIPE
4 t goat cheese
4 t sun-dried tomatoes, well-drained
zest of one lemon

BASIC STUFFED BURGER RECIPE
1 lb ground turkey, chicken, pork or sirloin
1/4 cup egg white substitute or 1 egg
1/4 cup oat bran

Instructions:

1. Mix all ingredients by hand, careful not to handle too much. Season with salt and pepper.
2. Quarter off the meat and separate into 4 large patties about 1/2- inch thick.
3. Place all stuffing ingredients in the center of each patty and fold in the sides to cover filling and form an enclosed 1-inch thick patty.
4. Prepare grill or grill pan and spray with cooking spray. Grill for approximately 5 minutes per side.

Makes 4 burgers

Stuffed Burgers

STUFFED GREEK TURKEY BURGERS
BASIC STUFFED BURGER RECIPE
1/2 lb ground turkey
2 T red onion, chopped
2 T red bell pepper, chopped
2 T fresh parsley, chopped
1 t lemon zest
1/4 t garlic powder
2 t goat or feta cheese

Stuff with goat cheese.

Serve with Cucumber Yogurt Sauce.

Cucumber-Yogurt Sauce
3 oz fat free Greek yogurt
2 T cucumber, peeled, seeded and chopped
1 t red onion, chopped
1 t red bell pepper, chopped
1 t fresh parsley, chopped
a pinch of salt, pepper and garlic powder

Mix all ingredients well and refrigerate until ready to use.

Stuffed Burgers

BACON, JALAPENO & CHEDDAR BURGERS
BASIC STUFFED BURGER RECIPE
1/4 cup Real Bacon Bits
1 jalapeno, seeded and finely chopped
2 mini Laughing Cow® Light Babybel, cut into small cubes

Stuff with bacon, jalapeno and cheese.

HAWAIIAN BURGERS
BASIC STUFFED BURGER RECIPE
2 oz turkey ham, cut into small cubes
2 oz low or fat free cheddar, sliced
1 slice of onion, grilled separately
1 slice of pineapple, grilled separately

Stuff with ham and cheese; top with onion and pineapple.

Pastas

BASIC PASTA RECIPE

2 packages Tofu Shirataki noodles or
1 box whole grain or whole wheat pasta
salt

Cook pasta as directed on package or boil Shirataki noodles for 4 minutes and drain well.

Prepare sauce as instructed and serve over pasta.

Serves 4

BASIC PASTA SAUCE RECIPE

1 cup onion, chopped
4 garlic cloves, thinly sliced
2 T tomato paste
1/2 cup dry red wine or 2 T balsamic vinegar
1 T Splenda®
1 T chopped fresh or 2 t dried basil
1/4 t dried oregano
2 T chopped fresh or 1 T dried parsley
2 15 oz cans diced tomatoes or 1 32 oz can of plum tomatoes, chopped
1/2 t red pepper flakes

1. Heat oil in a saucepan over medium-high heat. Add onion and garlic and sauté 5 minutes. Add tomato paste and cook for one minute.
2. Stir the rest of the ingredients and bring to a boil.
3. Reduce heat to medium, and cook, uncovered for about 15 minutes.

Makes 3 cups.

SCAMPI FRA DIAVOLO
BASIC PASTA RECIPE
*2 cups **BASIC PASTA SAUCE RECIPE** Or 1 15 oz can diced tomatoes*
4 cloves garlic, crushed
1/2 t dried basil
1/2 t dried oregano
1/4 t red pepper flakes
1 lb shrimp, deveined and peeled

1. Sauté garlic in a bit of cooking spray for 2 minutes. Add tomato sauce, basil, oregano and red pepper flakes and cook for 20 minutes, adding the shrimp in the last 2 or 3 minutes. Season with salt.
2. Toss with pasta and serve.

24

Pastas

LOBSTER CHOW MEIN
BASIC PASTA RECIPE
1/4 cup low sodium soy sauce
1/2 onion, cut into thin slices
1 8 oz package of mushrooms, sliced
1 cup broccoli florets
1/4 lb snow peas
3 oz water chestnuts, sliced
2 cloves garlic, minced
1 T oyster sauce
1/2 t chili paste (optional)
1 lb cooked lobster meat

1. Place the noodles in a non stick pan with about half the soy sauce and fry until the noodles have browned a bit. Remove from skillet and set aside.
2. Sauté the vegetables in a bit of olive oil spray and the other half of the soy sauce.
3. When vegetables are done, add the pasta back in, along with the garlic, oyster sauce and chili paste. Add the lobster in at the last minute, just long enough to warm.

PENNE BOLOGNESE
BASIC PASTA RECIPE
2 cups **BASIC PASTA SAUCE RECIPE** or 1 15 oz can diced tomatoes
1 medium onion, chopped
2 cloves of garlic, crushed
1/4 cup dry red wine
2 turkey Italian sausages, removed from casing
1/2 lb ground sirloin
1/2 lb ground lean pork
1/4 cup fat free half and half

1. Sauté onion in a bit of cooking spray for about 8 minutes, adding the garlic in the last minute. Add wine and cook until reduced by half.
2. Then add the tomato sauce, bring to a boil and then reduce the heat to low. Add all the meat and stir constantly until meat has broken down and there are no chunks. Sauce should be thick, but not chunky.
3. Cook for an hour finishing with the half and half just before the hour is up. Serve over pasta.

Pastas

ANGEL HAIR WITH TURKEY ITALIAN SAUSAGE AND VEGETABLES

BASIC PASTA RECIPE
2 cups BASIC PASTA SAUCE RECIPE or 1 15 oz can diced tomatoes
1 lb hot turkey Italian sausage
1 small red onion, sliced
1 red bell pepper, diced
1 garlic clove, minced
1 8 oz package of mushrooms, sliced
2 small zucchinis, halved lengthwise and sliced
2 T dried parsley
1 t dried basil
1/2 cup light or fat free sour cream
1/2 t red pepper flakes

1. Remove casings from sausage and brown with onion, pepper and garlic for 5-10 minutes, or until meat is cooked. Add mushrooms and sauté 5 more minutes. Stir in tomato sauce, zucchini, parsley, basil and pasta, cover and cook over medium-low heat for another 5 minutes.
2. Remove from heat and stir in the sour cream, season with salt and pepper flakes and reheat over medium-low heat for 3 minutes or until hot.

LINGUINE PESCATORE

BASIC PASTA RECIPE
1 cup BASIC PASTA SAUCE RECIPE or 1 8 oz can tomato sauce
1/2 cup white wine
3 cloves garlic, crushed
1/4 lb mussels
1/2 lb Manila clams
1/2 lb shrimp, peeled and deveined
1/4 lb calamari tubes, cut into rings

1. Sauté garlic in a bit of cooking spray. Add the wine and reduce by half, about 10 minutes.
2. Add tomato sauce and all the seafood, cover and cook about 5 minutes, throwing away any clams or mussels that don't open.
3. Season with salt and pepper and serve over pasta.

Baked Dishes

BASIC BAKED DISH OR PASTA RECIPE

2 packages Tofu Shirataki noodles or
1/2 box whole grain or whole wheat pasta
salt

Bake Instructions: Cook pasta as directed on the box or boil Shirataki noodles for 4 minutes and drain well. Coat a casserole dish with cooking spray. Mix all ingredients together and bake dish at 375 for 25 minutes. Let dish set for 10 minutes before serving.

Serves 4

BACON AND CHEESEBURGER PASTA BAKE
BASIC BAKED PASTA RECIPE
*3 cups **BASIC PASTA SAUCE RECIPE** or 2 15 oz can diced tomatoes and 1 8 oz can tomato sauce*
1 medium onion, chopped
2 turkey Italian sausages, removed from casing
1/2 lb ground sirloin
3 cloves garlic, sliced
2 T tomato paste
1 t Splenda®
1 T chopped fresh or 1 t dried parsley
1 T chopped fresh or 1 t dried basil
1 T chopped fresh or 1 t dried oregano
1/2 cup Real Bacon Bits
1/2 cup skim or fat free mozzarella cheese, shredded
2 T grated Parmesan cheese
salt and pepper and red pepper flakes

1. Add onion, beef and sausage to a skillet and cook 5 minutes. Add garlic and cook another minute. Add the tomato paste, tomato sauce, herbs, Splenda® and season with salt and pepper. Simmer for 20 minutes, adding half the bacon in the last minute.
2. Add half the noodles to the casserole dish, add half the sauce, and then repeat. Top with cheeses and the rest of the bacon-See Bake Instructions

Baked Dishes

CHICKEN, MUSHROOM, SPINACH AND ZUCCHINI LASAGNE

*3 cups **BASIC PASTA SAUCE RECIPE***
1 8 oz package sliced mushrooms
4 medium zucchini, sliced 1/4-inch thick
1 rotisserie chicken, all the meat removed and shredded
1 cup fat free ricotta cheese
2 cups fat free cottage cheese
2 10 oz boxes of frozen spinach, thawed and well dried in paper towels
1 cup fat free or skim mozzarella cheese, shredded
1/2 cup Parmesan cheese, grated

1. In a skillet, brown the mushrooms. Add the sauce to the skillet and heat for 15 minutes. Season with salt and red pepper flakes.
2. Spray a large casserole dish with cooking spray. Spread 4 tablespoons of sauce on the bottom and follow with half the zucchini, ricotta, cottage cheese, chicken and all the spinach. Top with half the mozzarella and half the sauce. Repeat the zucchini, chicken, cheeses and sauce and finish with the Parmesan.
3. Bake at 350 for 25-30 minutes, or until bubbly. Let set 10 minutes.

CHICKEN, BROCCOLI AND SUN-DRIED TOMATO PASTA BAKE

BASIC BAKED PASTA RECIPE
*1 cup **BASIC PASTA SAUCE RECIPE** or 1 8 oz can tomato sauce*
1/2 cup low fat ricotta cheese
1 cup cooked chicken breast, cubed
2 cups broccoli florets
1/2 cup sun-dried tomatoes, drained well
1 t red pepper flakes

1. Add the ricotta cheese to the pasta sauce and cook for 5 minutes, seasoning with salt and red pepper flakes -See Bake Instructions

Baked Dishes

BEEF, MUSHROOM, ZUCCHINI AND SPINACH BAKE

BASIC BAKED DISH RECIPE
1 cup skim milk
1 t cornstarch mixed with 1 T water
1/2 cup fat free mozzarella cheese, shredded
1/2 lb ground sirloin
1 leek, white part only, sliced
4 oz fresh mushrooms, sliced
1 clove garlic, crushed
1 small zucchini, quartered lengthwise and chopped
1 10 oz package frozen chopped spinach, thawed and squeezed dry
1 t dried oregano
a pinch of nutmeg
1/4 cup oat bran
1/2 cup fat free cottage cheese

1. Whisk the milk over medium heat until warm and add the cornstarch mixture whisking continuously until the sauce thickens, about 3-5 minutes. Add the cheese and whisk until mixed in. Pour into a large bowl and set aside.
2. In a skillet, brown beef, leeks, mushrooms and garlic over medium heat for 5 minutes and drain-See Bake Instructions

29

SHRIMP, PORCINI MUSHROOMS AND ARTICHOKES BAKE

1 cup BASIC PASTA SAUCE RECIPE or 1 8 oz can tomato sauce
8 oz porcini mushrooms
2 cloves garlic, minced
1/4 cup white wine
1/2 lb shrimp, peeled and deveined
1 14 oz can of artichoke hearts, quartered
1 t dried oregano
1/4 cup fresh basil, torn

1. Using the liquid from the artichokes, sauté mushrooms and garlic.
2. Add wine and reduce by half.
3. Add shrimp, tomato sauce, artichokes and oregano. Simmer for 5 minutes, stirring occasionally. Season with salt, pepper and basil-See Bake Instructions

Baked Dishes

1. Bake squash cut side down on a cookie sheet for 20-30 minutes at 375. Remove from skin, drain well and set aside
2. Meanwhile, sauté turkey and bell pepper in a bit of olive oil spray for about 8 minutes. Add tomato sauce and simmer for 15 minutes-See Bake Instructions.

SPAGHETTI SQUASH LASAGNE CASSEROLE

3 cups ***BASIC PASTA SAUCE RECIPE***
1 medium spaghetti squash, halved and seeded
1 lb ground turkey
1 red bell pepper, chopped
2 cups low or fat free cottage cheese
1 cup low or fat free mozzarella cheese, shredded
1/4 cup Parmesan cheese

Baked Dishes

CHICKEN SAUSAGE, PUMPKIN AND SPINACH BAKE
BASIC BAKED DISH RECIPE
1 cup skim milk
1 t cornstarch mixed with 1 T water
1/2 cup fat free mozzarella cheese, shredded
2 chicken sausages, casings removed
1/2 small onion, chopped
1 clove garlic, crushed
2 cups pumpkin, peeled and cut into 1/4-inch cubes
1 10 oz package frozen chopped spinach, thawed and squeezed dry
1 t dried basil
a pinch of nutmeg
1/4 cup oat bran
1/2 cup fat free cottage cheese

1. Whisk the milk over medium heat until warm and add the cornstarch mixture whisking continuously until the sauce thickens, about 3-5 minutes. Add the cheese and whisk until mixed in. Pour into a large bowl and set aside.
2. In a skillet, brown sausage, onions, and garlic over medium heat for 5 minutes and drain-See Bake Instructions

TURKEY SAUSAGE AND CAULIFLOWER PASTA BAKE
BASIC BAKED PASTA RECIPE
2 turkey Italian sausage, casings removed, browned and crumbled
2 cups cauliflower florets, par-boiled with noodles in the last few minutes
6 oz skim or fat free mozzarella, shredded
2 T Parmesan cheese, finely shredded
8 oz low or fat free sour cream
1 t red pepper flakes

See Bake Instructions

Baked Dishes

2. In a skillet, brown the, ground sirloin and sausage. Add the sauce to the skillet and heat for 15 minutes. Season with salt and red pepper flakes.

3. Spray a large casserole with cooking spray. Spread 4 tablespoons of sauce on the bottom and spread half the noodles or cauliflower (or both) on top of it. Dot with half of the ricotta and cottage cheese. Top with half the mozzarella. Cover with half the sauce. Repeat the noodles/cauliflower, cheeses and sauce layers and top with the Parmesan.

4. Bake at 350 for 25-30 minutes, or until bubbly.

BAKED ZITI
3 cups ***BASIC PASTA SAUCE RECIPE***
BASIC BAKED PASTA RECIPE *or 4 cups cauliflower florets or half of each*
1 lb ground sirloin
3 chicken Italian sausages, casings removed
1 cup fat free ricotta cheese
2 cups fat free cottage cheese
1 cup fat free or skim mozzarella cheese, shredded
1/2 cup Parmesan cheese, grated

1. Boil the cauliflower in some salted water until al dente, about 3 minutes. Remove with a slotted spoon and rough chop it. Cook the noodles in the boiling water as instructed on the box, drain and set aside.

Baked Dishes

TURKEY SAUSAGE LASAGNE RECIPE

*3 cups **BASIC PASTA SAUCE RECIPE***
3 turkey sausage links, removed from casings
1 1/2 cups egg substitute
8 oz low fat cottage cheese
4 oz low fat ricotta cheese
4 oz skim milk mozzarella, thinly sliced
2 T finely shredded Parmesan cheese

1. Brown the sausage in a sauté pan, drain and add the pasta sauce. Cook for 20 minutes while you prepare the "noodles".
2. Heat 2 sauté pans, either the same size or one slightly smaller than the other, and spray with cooking spray.

3. Pour 3/4 cup of egg whites in the smaller pan and season with salt, pepper and red pepper flakes. Once the egg is almost cooked through, flip and transfer to second sauté pan and begin to make your second
4. Once you have two "noodles" made you can get rid of the smaller pan and begin to assemble the lasagne in the larger one.

Baked Dishes

6. Spoon half the sauce over the cheeses and repeat the layers, finishing with the Parmesan cheese.

5. Spoon a little of the sauce on the bottom of the pan, then add one of the "noodles", half the cottage, ricotta and mozzarella cheeses.

7. Bake at 375 for 35 minutes. The top should be nice and brown and the sauce bubbly. Let set 10-15 minutes before serving.

Shrimp

BASIC SHRIMP RECIPE

1 lb shrimp, peeled and deveined
3 cloves garlic, minced
1 t crushed red pepper flakes

Mix all ingredients together and keep refrigerated until ready to cook.

Serves 4

SHRIMP AND CALAMARI CEVICHE
BASIC SHRIMP RECIPE
1/2 lb calamari tubes, sliced into rings
3 limes, juiced
3 lemons, juiced
1/2 small red onion, finely chopped
1/4 cup red bell pepper, finely diced
1 small jalapeno, seeded and finely chopped
1/4 cup cilantro, chopped
1 avocado, diced
1 plum tomato, seeded and diced
2 dozen endive leaves

1. Mix the first 7 ingredients with the shrimp in a large bowl, cover and refrigerate 2 hours.
2. Add the avocado and tomato just before serving. Season with salt and pepper.
3. Serve ceviche with endive leaves for dipping.

LEMON GARLIC SHRIMP (Cover Recipe)
BASIC SHRIMP RECIPE
juice of one whole lemon
1/2 cup dry white wine
1 t lemon zest
2 T fresh parsley, chopped

1. Over low heat add the lemon juice, white wine, lemon zest, red pepper flakes to taste, and bring to a simmer.
2. Add the shrimp and cook for 3 minutes. Flip the shrimp, add the parsley and season with salt and pepper.
3. Cook for another 2-3 minutes, remove from heat and serve immediately.

Shrimp

GINGER PEPPER SHRIMP
BASIC SHRIMP RECIPE
2 t fresh ginger, minced
2 T white wine
2 T soy sauce
2 T rice wine vinegar
1 T honey or 1 t Splenda®
1 red bell pepper, sliced
1 t cornstarch mixed with 1 T water

1. Mix ginger, wine, soy sauce, vinegar and sweetener in a small bowl.
2. In a skillet, sauté the pepper over medium-high heat for 3 minutes; add the shrimp and cook for another minute, stirring constantly.
3. Pour the sauce over shrimp, cook for a minute and pour the cornstarch mixture over that. Cook for another 2 minutes, stirring well to coat the shrimp.

SWEET GINGER SHRIMP
BASIC SHRIMP RECIPE
1 T honey or 1 t Splenda®
1 t freshly grated ginger
1 t lemon juice
1 T sake
1 T green onion, finely chopped

1. Mix shrimp and all ingredients through the sake, in a large bowl. Cover and refrigerate for 1 hour.
2. Prepare grill or grill pan with a bit of olive spray over medium-high heat. Cook shrimp 2-3 minutes, depending on the size, flip and cook until other side is pink, about 2 more minutes. Season with salt, pepper and green onion.

Shrimp

FOUR PEPPER SHRIMP WITH SWEET AND SOUR PEPPER RELISH
BASIC SHRIMP RECIPE
2 t Splenda®
1 t chili powder
1/2 t ground pepper
1/2 t ancho chili powder
1/4 t chipotle chili powder
1 lb large shrimp, peeled and deveined
1/2 small onion, finely chopped
1/2 red bell pepper, finely chopped
1 clove garlic, finely chopped
1 T tomato paste
1 T red wine vinegar

1. In a bowl, mix the first six ingredients together well, with your hands. Refrigerate until ready to use.
2. In a skillet, sauté onion and bell pepper for five minutes, adding garlic in the last minute. Add the tomato paste and vinegar and cook for another minute. Place mixture on a plate.
3. Spray skillet with cooking spray and toss in the shrimp. Cook about 2-3 minutes, flip and cook for another minute or two.
4. Serve shrimp over relish.

37

SHRIMP WITH SUGAR SNAP PEAS
1/2 BASIC SHRIMP RECIPE
1/4 t salt
4 T water
1/2 t cornstarch
1 T dry white wine or sake
1 t soy sauce
1/2 t fish sauce (optional)
2 cloves garlic, minced
1/2 t fresh ginger, minced
4 oz sugar snap peas

1. Mix the first 6 ingredients in a small bowl and set aside.
2. Spray a skillet with cooking spray and add the garlic and ginger. Stir-fry for 1 minute and add the snap peas. Cook for 3 minutes. Add the shrimp and cook for another 3 minutes.
3. Add the sauce and stir-fry quickly for a few minutes until sauce thickens. If sauce gets too thick just add a little bit more water to the pan.

❧

Shrimp

VODKA SHRIMP AND SCALLOPS
BASIC SHRIMP RECIPE
1/2 small onion, finely chopped
1/2 cup vodka
1 14 oz can crushed tomatoes
1/2 cup fat free half and half
1/2 lb bay scallops, halved if large

1. Cut the shrimp in half. Sauté the onion for 5 minutes, add vodka and cook until reduced to half. Add tomatoes and continue to cook another 10 minutes, until some of the juices are gone. Add the half and half and season with salt and pepper.
2. Add the seafood and cook for about 3-4 minutes, or until done.

BARBECUED CREOLE SHRIMP
BASIC SHRIMP RECIPE
1/2 cup Worcestershire sauce
juice and zest from one lemon
2 T Creole seasoning
2 cloves garlic, finely chopped
1 1/2 cup low sodium chicken broth with 1 T cornstarch, whisked together

1. Over high heat, cook the shrimp, Worcestershire, lemon juice and zest, seasoning and garlic. Cook until shrimp is pink, about 1-2 minutes on each side.
2. Turn the heat down to medium and add the chicken broth and cornstarch mixture. Cook until sauce thickens, about 3-5 minutes. If you need more time to thicken the sauce, don't overcook the shrimp, just remove them and turn the sauce up, then pour the sauce over the shrimp and serve.

SHRIMP AND CUCUMBER SALAD RECIPE
BASIC SHRIMP RECIPE
1/2 large English cucumber, peeled, sliced and quartered
1/4 cup unseasoned rice wine vinegar
dash of soy sauce
1 T minced fresh chives
1 t finely diced jalapeno, seeded (optional)

1. Sauté the shrimp for 3-4 minutes in a skillet, cool and cut in half.
2. Toss all ingredients together and season with pepper.
3. Let marinade for at least 10 minutes in the refrigerator. Serve cold.

Fish

BASIC WHITE FISH RECIPE

4 6oz cod or other white fish fillets

Broil Instructions: Spray fish with cooking spray and broil fish about 8 minutes, about 6 inches from the heat until nice and flaky and opaque in the center.

Bake En Papillote Instructions: Spray 4 12-inch squares of parchment paper with cooking spray. Place fish and a quarter of the vegetables in the center of each piece, top with sauce and fresh herb sprigs. Fold opposite corners in, followed by other two opposite corners and pinch shut. Bake at 500 for 11 minutes. Serve entire package on individual plates.

Serves 4

BROILED COD IN LIME AND JALAPENO SAUCE
BASIC WHITE FISH RECIPE
1/2 t salt
1/2 t garlic powder
1 t lemon pepper
1/4 cup low or fat free sour cream
1/2 t Dijon mustard
2 t jalapeno, seeded and finely chopped
1 t lime juice
1 t lime zest

1. Season fillets with salt, garlic powder and lemon pepper.
2. Mix sour cream, Dijon, jalapeno, lime juice and zest in a small bowl. Spread a thin layer over the top of each fillet. See-Broil Instructions.

COD EN PAPILLOTE WITH TOMATOES AND ASPARAGUS
BASIC WHITE FISH RECIPE
1 t lemon pepper
2 cloves of garlic, finely chopped
1 t salt
1/4 cup lemon juice
1 t lemon zest
3 T white wine
16 asparagus spears, trimmed
16 grape tomatoes
2 t lemon thyme, chopped plus 4 sprigs
8 sprigs parsley

1. Season fish with lemon pepper.
2. Mix garlic, salt, lemon juice and zest and wine in a small bowl. See-Bake En Papillote Instructions.

Fish

MISO GLAZED COD
BASIC WHITE FISH RECIPE
1/4 cup sake
1/4 cup rice vinegar
1/4 cup miso (soy paste)
2 T Brown Sugar Blend Splenda® or 1 t Splenda®
1 T soy sauce
green onions, chopped

Mix sake, vinegar, miso, Splenda® and soy in a shallow baking dish, add fish and cover. Marinate for at least 2 and up to 6 hours. See-Broil Instructions. Garnish with green onion.

40

Fish

BASIC GRILLED SALMON FILLET RECIPE

4 6oz salmon fillets, with skin
1 T lemon pepper

Grill Instructions: Season salmon with lemon pepper. Spray grill and salmon with cooking spray. Grill flesh side down for 3 minutes, rotate 45 degrees for diamond grill marks, then flip and cook skin side down for another 5 minutes or until done.

Serves 4

GRILLED SALMON
WITH CUCUMBER DILL DIP
BASIC SALMON RECIPE
1 T lemon zest
2 T lemon juice

Sprinkle salmon with lemon zest and juice. See-Grill Instructions. Serve with Cucumber and Dill Dip.

Cucumber and Dill Dip
8 oz fat free sour cream
1 small cucumber, peeled, quartered, seeded and sliced
2 T fresh dill, chopped
1 T green onion, finely chopped
1 T lemon juice

Mix all ingredients and season with salt and pepper.

GRILLED WHISKEY & LEMON SALMON
BASIC SALMON RECIPE
1/4 cup Whiskey
1/4 cup fresh lemon juice
zest of one lemon
1/4 cup low sodium soy sauce
3 T Brown Sugar Blend Splenda® or 2 t Splenda®
1/4 cup green onion, chopped
2 cloves garlic, chopped
3 T fresh chives, chopped

Combine first 7 ingredients in a large resealable plastic bag, and add salmon to bag. Seal and marinate in refrigerator for 1 1/2 hours, turning bag occasionally-See Grill Instructions. Garnish with chives.

Chicken Breasts and Thighs

BASIC CHICKEN BREAST & THIGHS RECIPE

4 boneless, skinless chicken breasts or thighs or a mixture

Pan-Fry Instructions: Pound chicken between two pieces of plastic wrap until about 1/2-inch thick. Season with salt and pepper. Cook chicken in a skillet sprayed with cooking spray for about 5 minutes on each side. Remove and keep warm on a plate covered with foil.

Braise Stove-top Instructions: Brown chicken in a bit of olive oil spray, pour liquid in pot, cover and simmer for 30-35 minutes.

Oven Braise Instructions: Combine all sauce ingredients. Pour half the sauce over the chicken and bake at 400 for 30-40 minutes, basting occasionally with extra sauce, adding water if necessary. Serve chicken with a bit of the extra sauce.

Serves 4

CHICKEN WITH LEMON AND CAPERS

BASIC CHICKEN BREAST & THIGH RECIPE
1 leek, cleaned and sliced, white part only
2 cloves garlic, minced
1/2 cup low sodium chicken broth
1/4 cup white wine
juice and zest of one lemon
2 T fresh rosemary, finely chopped
2 T capers, drained

1. See Pan-Fry Instructions. Sauté the leeks and garlic in a bit of cooking spray for about 3 minutes.
2. Add the broth, wine, lemon juice and juices from the chicken on the plate and cook on medium-high for another 5 minutes, reducing sauce by half.
3. Add lemon zest, rosemary and capers and season with salt and pepper.
4. Add chicken back to pan and cook 3 minutes to warm chicken.

Chicken Breasts and Thighs

CHICKEN WITH ROASTED PEPPERS, ARTICHOKE HEARTS AND KALAMATA OLIVES

BASIC CHICKEN BREAST & THIGH RECIPE
2 cloves garlic, minced
1/4 cup white wine
1 16 oz can diced tomatoes, with juices
4 oz roasted red peppers, drained and chopped
1 16 oz can quartered artichoke hearts, drained
1/4 cup kalamata olives
2 T fresh basil, chopped
red pepper flakes

1. See Pan-Fry Instructions. Sauté the garlic in a bit of cooking spray for about 1 minute.
2. Add the wine, tomatoes, peppers, artichokes, olives and juices from the chicken on the plate and cook on medium-high for another 5 minutes, reducing sauce by half. Add basil and season with salt and peppers.
3. Add chicken back to pan and cook 3 minutes to warm chicken.

CHICKEN BREASTS WITH MAPLE MUSTARD SAUCE

BASIC CHICKEN BREAST & THIGH RECIPE
2 T red onion, chopped
6 T sugar free maple syrup
1/4 cup Dijon mustard
1 T water
1 t fresh dill, chopped
1 t orange rind, grated

1. See Pan-Fry Instructions. Add onion to the skillet and cook for 3 minutes.
2. Add syrup, Dijon, water, dill and orange rind and cook until reduced, about 2 minutes.
3. Season sauce with salt and pepper and pour over chicken.

Chicken Breasts and Thighs

CHICKEN FLORENTINE
BASIC CHICKEN BREAST & THIGH RECIPE
1 shallot, finely chopped
2 cloves garlic, minced
1/2 cup low sodium chicken broth
1/4 cup white wine
1/2 cup fat free half and half
1 T fresh parsley, chopped
1 t cornstarch mixed with 1 T water
2 8 oz packages frozen cut spinach, thawed and well-drained

CHICKEN THIGHS IN SPICY CILANTRO SAUCE
BASIC CHICKEN BREAST & THIGH RECIPE
1 small onion, sliced
1/4 cup water
3 T rice vinegar
2-3 T soy sauce
a bunch of cilantro, chopped
2 large garlic cloves, minced
2 green onion, chopped
1/2 jalapeno, seeded and chopped
1/2-1 t chili paste
1 t olive oil
1/2 t Splenda®

Put all ingredients in a blender and process until smooth. See Oven Braise Instructions.

1. See Pan-Fry Instructions. Sauté the shallots and garlic in a bit of cooking spray for about 3 minutes.
2. Add the broth, wine and juices from the chicken on the plate and cook on medium-high for another 5 minutes, reducing sauce by half.
3. Add half and half and parsley and season with salt and pepper. Cook for another 5 minutes, adding the cornstarch in the last minute.
4. Add the spinach and chicken. Cook 3-5 minutes to warm.

44

Chicken Breasts and Thighs

TEQUILA-LIME CHICKEN THIGHS
BASIC CHICKEN BREAST & THIGH RECIPE
1/2 cup lime juice
1/4 cup tequila
1 T agave syrup or 1 t Splenda®
1 t lime zest
1 t ground cumin
1/2 serrano chili, finely diced
1 t cornstarch

1. Mix all the ingredients down to the cornstarch, in a bowl- See Oven Braise Instructions:
2. Once meat is cooked, drain the sauce into a saucepan and add the cornstarch. Cook for 5 minutes, until thick. Pour over chicken and serve.

CUBAN SPICY SWEET GLAZED CHICKEN
BASIC CHICKEN BREAST & THIGH RECIPE
1/2 cup unsweetened apple juice
4 T lime juice
1 t Worcestershire sauce
1 t cider vinegar
1/2 t smoked paprika
1/4 t cumin
1 jalapeno, seeded and chopped

See Pan-Fry Instructions. Mix all sauce ingredients together in the skillet. Add the chicken back to the pan to warm and serve with sauce.

BALSAMIC CHICKEN
BASIC CHICKEN BREAST & THIGH RECIPE
1 shallot, finely chopped
1 clove garlic, minced
1/4 cup low sodium chicken broth
1/4 cup red wine
1/4 cup honey or 2 t Splenda®
1/2 cup balsamic vinegar
1 t cornstarch mixed with 1 T water

1. See Pan-Fry Instructions. Sauté the shallot and garlic in a bit of cooking spray for about 3 minutes.
2. Add the broth, wine, honey, vinegar and juices from the chicken on the plate and cook on medium-high for another 5 minutes, reducing sauce by half. Season with salt and pepper.
3. Add cornstarch mixture and cook for 3 minutes until sauce thickens. Add the chicken and cook 3-5 minutes to warm chicken. Serve with sauce.

Chicken Breasts and Thighs

FILIPINO CHICKEN THIGHS
BASIC CHICKEN BREAST & THIGH RECIPE
1/2 onion, chopped
1/3 cup water
1/4 cup white vinegar
1/4 cup soy sauce
2 bay leaves
2 cloves garlic, minced
2 T jalapeno, sliced thinly
1 t cornstarch mixed with 1 T water

1. See Braise Stove-top Instructions. In a skillet, brown onions in a bit of olive oil spray.
2. Add water, vinegar, soy sauce, bay leaves, garlic, and pepper and stir. Bring liquid to a boil, add the cornstarch, and simmer for 3 to 5 minutes, or until thickened.
3. Add the chicken and season with salt and pepper. Braise, covered for 30 more minutes. Serve chicken with sauce, garnishing with chili pepper.

COQ AU VIN
BASIC CHICKEN BREAST & THIGH RECIPE
use 6 chicken thighs
2 T cornstarch
2 8 oz packages white mushrooms, quartered
4 large carrots, sliced
6 slices turkey bacon, chopped
2 T fresh parsley, chopped
1 T fresh thyme, chopped
1/2 cup dry red wine
1 cup low sodium chicken broth
1/2 cup tomato sauce
1 T tomato paste

See Braise Stove-top Instructions. Sprinkle cornstarch over chicken. Add mushrooms, carrots, bacon, parsley and thyme to pan and sauté 5 minutes. Stir in wine, broth, tomato sauce and tomato paste and cook another 10 minutes scraping up all the bits on the bottom of the pan. Braise, covered for 30 more minutes.

46

Chicken Breasts and Thighs

CHICKEN CACCIATORE
BASIC CHICKEN BREAST & THIGH RECIPE
1 cup mushrooms, sliced
1 red pepper, seeded and chopped
1 onion, chopped
1 carrot, peeled and chopped (optional)
1 28 oz can diced tomatoes, drained
1/2 cup red wine
2 t dried basil
2 T dried parsley
1 t dried oregano
red pepper flakes (optional)

See Braise Stove-top Instructions. Sauté the mushrooms for 5 minutes. Place chicken, pepper, onion, carrot, tomatoes, wine and seasonings in with the mushrooms.

CHILI-LIME CHICKEN THIGHS
BASIC CHICKEN BREAST & THIGH RECIPE
2/3 cup sugar free maple syrup
2/3 cup tomato sauce
1 T cider vinegar
1/2 t onion powder
1/2 t garlic powder
1 T brown sugar blend Splenda® or 1 t Splenda®
1/2 serrano chili, chopped
2 T Dijon
the juice and zest of one lime

Mix all the sauce ingredients in a bowl. See Oven Braise Instructions.

Pork

BASIC PORK TENDERLOIN OR CHOP RECIPE

1 pork tenderloin, about 1 1/4 lbs or
4 lean center cut pork chops

Serves 2-4

Grill Instructions: Grill over direct heat or in a grill pan until internal temperature reads 145 degrees, about 15 minutes for tenderloin, 5-7 minutes for chops. Let rest 5 minutes before cutting.

Tenderloin Broil Instructions: Place tenderloin on a shallow dish and broil, turning only once, 5 minutes a side. Baste with marinade and broil an additional 3 minutes a side. Let rest 5 minutes before cutting.

BARBECUE-RUBBED PORK CHOPS
BASIC PORK TENDERLOIN OR CHOP RECIPE

1 T Splenda® orBrown Sugar Blend Splenda®
1 t salt
1 t smoked paprika
1 t ancho chili powder
3/4 t garlic powder
3/4 t ground cumin
1/4 t dry mustard
1/8 t ground allspice
1/8 t chipotle chili powder

Combine first 9 ingredients and rub over both sides of pork- See Grill Instructions.

48

Pork

PORK CHOPS WITH TOMATO WINE SAUCE
BASIC PORK TENDERLOIN OR CHOP RECIPE

1/2 small onion, chopped
2 cloves garlic, minced
1 14 oz can tomato sauce
1 T capers
3 T white wine
1 t oregano
1 t basil
2 T parsley

1. See Grill Instructions. In a skillet, sauté onion for 5 minutes, then add the garlic and cook for one more minute. Add the rest of the ingredients, bring to a boil, then turn the heat down and simmer for 15 minutes.
2. Serve sauce over pork chops.

PORK CHOPS WITH TURKEY BACON AND BEER GRAVY
1/2 BASIC PORK TENDERLOIN OR CHOP RECIPE

2 slices of turkey bacon, diced
1 large shallot, finely chopped
1 T cornstarch
1/2 cup light beer
1/2 cup low sodium chicken broth
2 T fresh parsley, chopped

1. See Grill Instructions. In the meantime, add another spray of cooking oil to the skillet, add bacon and brown for 2 to 3 minutes.
2. Stir in the shallots and sauté with the bacon until soft, about 5 minutes. Sprinkle in cornstarch, stir for 1 minute, and then add the beer.
3. Cook until reduced by half, then whisk in the broth.
4. Season with salt and pepper and pour the gravy over the chops. Garnish with parsley.

Pork

CHIPOTLE PORK TENDERLOIN (Cover Recipe)
BASIC PORK TENDERLOIN OR CHOP RECIPE
2 chipotle peppers, chopped fine with 1 T adobo sauce
1/4 cup honey or 2 t Splenda®
1 t lime juice
1/2 t garlic powder
1 t minced onion
1 t smoked paprika
1/4 t liquid smoke

Mix all ingredients together and marinate for 1 and up to 6 hours. See-Broil Instructions.

Pork

PORK TENDERLOIN WITH CHILI SAUCE
BASIC PORK TENDERLOIN OR CHOP
RECIPE

juice from 3 small limes
3 T chili powder
1/4 t cumin
1 small onion, finely chopped
2 garlic cloves, minced
1 t Splenda®
1 t cornstarch
1 cup chicken broth

1. In a bowl, combine the lime juice, chili powder, cumin, onion, garlic, Splenda®, salt, and pepper. Spray the pork with cooking spray and add it to a resealable bag along with 2/3 of the marinade. Refrigerate for 2 hours. See-Broil Instructions.
2. To make the sauce, pour the reserved marinade into a small saucepan. Bring to a simmer over medium heat and cook for 5 minutes. Whisk the cornstarch into the chicken broth, and then whisk the mixture into the sauce. Simmer for 5 minutes, stirring occasionally until thickened. Cut the pork into thin slices and serve it with the Chili Sauce.

HONEY CHINESE BBQ PORK
BASIC PORK TENDERLOIN OR CHOP
RECIPE

2 cloves garlic, minced
1/2 t five spice powder
1 1/2 T soy sauce
1/2 t pepper (I used a bit of red pepper flakes too)
1 t salt
5 T honey or 3 t Splenda®

1. Slice pork tenderloin thinly and pound each slice until it's about 1/8-inch thin. Combine the rest of the ingredients and mix well. Put sauce and pork in a plastic baggie in the refrigerator for at least 5 hours to marinade. See Grill Instructions –shorten grill time to 2-3 minutes per side.
2. Reserve sauce for continual brushing while grilling.

Beef

BASIC STEAK RECIPE

2 lb top sirloin, London Broil or other lean steak

Grill Instructions: Prepare grill or grill pan and spray each side of the grill and steaks with cooking spray. Grill each side of steak for 5 minutes, for medium. Serve with sauce, if using.

Sauce Instructions: Season steaks with salt and pepper. Mix all sauce ingredients and place in a resealable baggie with the meat, reserving 1/4 cup for serving. Refrigerate for 8-24 hours.

Rub Instructions: Season steaks with salt and pepper. Mix all rub ingredients together. Rub into the meat and refrigerate, covered, for 20 minutes.

Serves 4

STEAK WITH MUSTARD PEPPERCORN RUB
BASIC STEAK RECIPE
1 t course-grainy brown mustard or Dijon mustard
2 t cracked peppercorns
2 t fresh tarragon, chopped

See-Rub and Grill Instructions

STEAK WITH TOMATO SALAD
BASIC STEAK RECIPE
1 shallot, finely chopped
2 t balsamic or sherry vinegar
2 medium tomatoes, chopped
1/2 cup basil leaves, torn
6 green olives, roughly chopped (optional)

Combine shallots and balsamic in bowl and let set for 15 minutes. Add the rest of the ingredients and serve immediately. See-Grill Instructions

Beef

STEAK FAJITAS
BASIC STEAK RECIPE

1/3 cup soy sauce
1/2 cup chopped cilantro
5 green onions, rough chopped
1/4 cup fresh lime juice
1/2 t ancho chili powder
1/2 t smoked paprika
2 T Brown Sugar Blend Splenda® or 1 1/2 t Splenda®
1 white onion, sliced
1 red bell pepper, sliced
iceberg lettuce leaves
fat free sour cream

1. Puree the first 7 ingredients in a food processor. Cut steak into strips. Pour mixture into a baggie and add the steak, onions and bell pepper. Marinate for an hour.
2. Remove the strips of meat from the marinade, reserve the marinade, and pat the meat dry with paper towels. See Grill Instructions-for both meat and vegetables. Serve meat and vegetables in lettuce cups and top with pico de gallo and sour cream.

53

Pico De Gallo
6 plum tomatoes, seeded and chopped
1/2 cup white onion, finely chopped
1/2-1 jalapeno, seeded and finely chopped
1/4 cup cilantro, chopped
1 T fresh lime juice
1/2 t garlic powder

Mix all ingredients together and refrigerate.

CUBAN SKIRT STEAK
BASIC STEAK RECIPE

1/3 cup fresh lime juice
1/4 cup soy sauce
1/2 t ground cumin
1 t dried oregano
1 t onion powder
1 t garlic powder
1/2 t chipotle chili powder
2 t lime zest
4 scallions, finely chopped
1/2 t red pepper flakes
2 T Splenda® brown sugar blend or 1 t Splenda®

Mix all the ingredients together with meat and marinate for 1 hour and up to overnight. See Grill Instructions.

Beef

STEAK RANCHERO
BASIC STEAK RECIPE
1/2 onion, sliced
1/2 red bell pepper
1/2 bunch cilantro

See Grill Instructions-for both meat and vegetables. Wilt cilantro on top of steak once flipped. Serve steak with vegetables, cilantro and ranchero salsa.

Ranchero Salsa
12 small tomatillos, washed, husked and cut in half
2 cloves of garlic, finely chopped
1 jalapeno
2 T tomato paste
1/3 cup cilantro, chopped
1/2 cup water
1 drop, liquid smoke (optional)
1/4 t cayenne pepper
1/4 t ancho chili powder
1/4 t chili powder
1 T paprika
1/2 small onion, finely chopped

Roast tomatillos, jalapeno and garlic in a skillet flipping once, until they are soft, about 15 minutes. Put the tomatillos, tomato paste, garlic, jalapeno, cilantro, water and liquid smoke in a food processor and process until smooth. Stir in seasonings and season with salt and pepper. Stir in the onion at the end. **54**

Beef

BEEF WITH BROCCOLI
BASIC STEAK RECIPE
1 T cornstarch
6 oz low sodium beef broth
1 T honey or 1 t Splenda®
2 T ponzu or soy sauce
1 clove garlic, minced
1/4 t fresh ginger, minced
2 cups broccoli, chopped

1. See Grill Instructions. Cut meat, against the grain, into strips.
2. Combine cornstarch, broth, Splenda® and ponzu in a small bowl. Add garlic, ginger and broccoli and cook for 1 minute.
3. Add sauce and continue to cook for 8 minutes, until sauce thickens, adding the meat back in, in the last 3 minutes. Serve with chili paste

MONGOLIAN BEEF
BASIC STEAK RECIPE
1/2 t ginger, minced
1 clove garlic, chopped
1/4 cup soy sauce
1/4 cup water
2 T Brown Sugar Blend Splenda® or 1 t Splenda®
2 T cornstarch
2 large green onions, cut greens into 2-inch strips, chop the whites
red pepper flakes to taste

1. See Grill Instructions. Cut meat, against the grain, into strips.
2. Add ginger and garlic to a skillet coated with cooking spray and quickly add soy sauce and water. Add sweetener to pan and let sauce thicken for a few minutes.
3. Add meat to the pan and sprinkle it with cornstarch. Add the sauce and simmer for another minute.
4. Add the green onions and red pepper flakes and cook for one last minute.

Beef

CHIMICHURRI FLANK STEAK
BASIC STEAK RECIPE
1 bunch of cilantro
3 cloves of garlic, chopped
3 T lemon juice
1/4 cup red wine vinegar
1 t salt
1/4 t pepper
1/4 t cayenne pepper
1 t paprika

Put all ingredients in a food processor and blend until combined. Put the sauce (reserving a few tablespoons) and the steak in a baggie and refrigerate for 1 hour-See Grill Instructions. Serve with the extra sauce.

BALSAMIC STEAK MARINADE
BASIC STEAK RECIPE
1/2 cup balsamic vinegar
1/4 cup soy sauce
3 T garlic, crushed
1 t Splenda® or 2 T honey or agave syrup
1 t olive oil
2 t pepper
1 t Worcestershire sauce
1 t onion powder
1/2 t salt
1/2 t liquid smoke flavoring
1/4 t cayenne pepper

Combine all sauce ingredients and pour over steaks. Refrigerate, covered, for up to 24 hours-See Grill Instructions.

Meatloaf

BASIC MEATLOAF RECIPE

*1 lb ground turkey, pork or beef or a combination of
any 3*
1/2 small onion, finely chopped
1/4 cup egg white substitute or 1 egg
2 T fresh parsley, chopped
2 garlic cloves, chopped
1/4 cup oat bran

Serves 4

Bake Instructions:

1. Place all wet ingredients together in bowl and
sprinkle all dry ingredients over the wet.
2. Combine all ingredients with hands, trying not to
handle too much. Place meat mixture in pan(s).
3. If baking with the sauce, combine sauce
ingredients and brush sauce over meatloaf.
4. If serving sauce with the meatloaf, prepare sauce
while it is baking.
5. For individual cupcake sized meatloaves, bake at
350 for 20 minutes. For two mini loaves, bake,
uncovered, at 350 for 30 minutes. For one large
meatloaf, bake at 350 for 1 hour. Let stand 10
minutes before slicing.

CHIPOTLE TURKEY MEATLOAF
BASIC MEATLOAF RECIPE
*2 chipotle peppers, chopped fine with 1 T adobo
sauce*
1/2 cup fresh cilantro, chopped
2 T fresh parsley, chopped
1/4 cup tomato sauce
1/2 t ground cumin
1/2 t dried oregano
1/4 t dried basil

Baked Sauce Ingredients:
1/4 cup tomato sauce
1 T tomato paste
1 t chipotle hot sauce

See-Bake Instructions

Meatloaf

BEEF MEATLOAF WITH MUSHROOM GRAVY
BASIC MEATLOAF RECIPE
2 T tomato paste
4 T sun-dried tomatoes, chopped

See-Bake Instructions

Separate Sauce Ingredients:
1 8 oz package mushrooms, sliced
1 cup low sodium beef broth
1/4 t Dijon mustard
1 t fresh thyme
1 T cornstarch

Sauté the mushrooms in a bit of olive oil spray. Whisk the beef broth, Dijon, thyme, and cornstarch in a separate bowl until smooth. Add to skillet and cook until thick, about 5 minutes. Season with salt and pepper. Serve over meatloaf.

Squash Pancakes

BASIC SQUASH PANCAKE RECIPE

2 cups shredded zucchini, pumpkin or butternut squash
1/2 cup ground turkey, sausage, beef or chicken, crumbled and browned
1/4 cup oat bran
2 eggs, lightly beaten

Instructions: Mix all the ingredients together until blended, adding the eggs at the very end. Making 8 pancakes out of the mixture. Fry them in a bit of cooking spray over medium heat, about 5-6 minutes per side and season with salt and pepper. Mix all the sauce ingredients together and refrigerate until ready to use. Serve over pancakes.

Serves 4

PUMPKIN, BACON AND LEEK PANCAKES
BASIC SQUASH PANCAKE RECIPE
4 slices turkey bacon, chopped and browned
1 leek, white part only, chopped and sautéed with the bacon
2 T mushrooms, chopped
2 T bell pepper, chopped
1/4 cup fresh parsley, chopped or 1 t dried

See-Instructions

ZUCCHINI AND CHICKEN SAUSAGE PANCAKES
BASIC SQUASH PANCAKE RECIPE
2 green onions, finely chopped
3 T Parmesan cheese, finely shredded
1/4 cup fresh parsley, chopped or 2 t dried

Sauce Ingredients:
1/2 cup fat free sour cream
1/4 cup fresh parsley, chopped or 1 t dried
salt and pepper

See-Instructions

Squash Pancakes

BUTTERNUT SQUASH AND GROUND TURKEY PANCAKES
BASIC SQUASH PANCAKE RECIPE
1 small red onion, finely chopped
3 T feta cheese, crumbled
1/4 cup fresh oregano, chopped or 2 t dried
1 t red pepper flakes

Sauce Ingredients:
1/2 cup fat free Greek yogurt
1/4 cup fresh oregano, chopped or 1 t dried
salt and pepper

See-Instructions

Chilis/Stews

BASIC CHILI/STEW RECIPE

1 lb. ground or cubed meat or 2 chicken breasts, or 1 pork tenderloin, cubed
1 onion, chopped

Instructions: Sauté meat with onion and/or garlic and the rest of the vegetables. Stir in tomatoes or any liquids and all seasonings. Simmer, covered, for 30 minutes. If using cornstarch, remove cover, stir in cornstarch mixture and cook for another 5-10 minutes, or until desired thickness.

Serves 4

TURKEY AND PUMPKIN CHILI
BASIC CHILI/STEW RECIPE
1 red bell pepper, chopped
1 celery stock, chopped
1 14-oz can diced tomatoes
1 cup pumpkin puree
2 cups fresh pumpkin, peeled and cubed
1 T chili powder
1 T paprika

See Instructions. Garnish with shredded fat free cheese and fat free sour cream.

MUSHROOM AND JALAPENO PORK CHILI
BASIC CHILI/STEW RECIPE
1/2 jalapeno, chopped (seeded if you prefer less spicy)
2 T dried red bell pepper
4 oz sliced mushrooms
1 16 oz can diced or crushed tomatoes
1 cup water
1 t paprika
1/4 t chili powder
1/4 t cayenne pepper
1 t cornstarch mixed with 2 T water

See Instructions.

Chilis/Stews

GREEK CHILI
BASIC CHILI/STEW RECIPE

1 red bell pepper, chopped
1 green bell pepper chopped
2 15 oz cans diced tomatoes
1 15 oz can tomato sauce
1 15 oz can garbanzo beans
1-3 t chili powder
1 T paprika
1 t garlic powder
1 t cayenne pepper
1/4 t ancho chili powder

Garnish:
fat free plain Greek yogurt
feta cheese
red onion, chopped
red bell pepper, chopped
jalapeno, chopped
1 T toasted pine nuts
1 T kalamata olives

See Instructions. Garnish with any, or all of the suggested garnishes.

CHICKEN CHILI
BASIC CHILI/STEW RECIPE

1/2 red bell pepper, diced
1 8 oz package of whole mushrooms, quartered
2 10 oz cans of diced tomatoes with green chilis
1 t ancho chili powder
1 t chili powder
1 t cayenne pepper
1/2 t dried oregano
1 T cornstarch in 2 T water

See Instructions.

Chilis/Stews

GUINNESS® BEEF PIE WITH CAULIFLOWER MASH
BASIC CHILI/STEW RECIPE

2 large carrots, cut into 1/4-inch rounds
3 large cloves garlic, minced
2 sprigs fresh thyme
1 bottle Guinness®
1 cup lower sodium beef broth
1 T cornstarch in 2 T water

Topping:
1 head cauliflower, steamed
1 T fresh chives, chopped
2 T fat free cream cheese
1/4-1/2 cup chicken broth, heated

1. See Instructions-adjust cooking time to 2-3 hours.
2. Mash the cauliflower, chives and the cream cheese and slowly add the chicken broth until mashed potatoes consistency. Season with salt and pepper.
3. Pour the beef into a casserole dish and pipe the cauliflower over the stew.

Chilis/Stews

MEDITERRANEAN BEEF STEW
BASIC CHILI/STEW RECIPE

1 clove garlic, minced

2 cups water

3 T red wine vinegar

6 oz tomato paste

1/2 t chili paste or 1/2 t chili powder

1/2 t hot paprika

1/2 t oregano

1/2 t fresh thyme

1/2 t cinnamon

1/8 t cloves

1 T cornstarch mixed with 2 T water

See Instructions.

LAMB STEW
BASIC CHILI/STEW RECIPE

3 cloves garlic, minced

5 carrots, peeled and cut into 1-inch pieces

1 T tomato paste

1/2 cup red wine

4 cups low sodium beef broth

1 T cornstarch mixed with 2 T water

1. See Instructions-adjust cooking time to 2 hours.

Oat Bran Muffins

BASIC FLOURLESS OAT BRAN MUFFIN RECIPE

8 T oat bran
1/2 cup egg white substitute or 2 eggs
1 T sugar free pudding powder (vanilla or chocolate depending on your tastes)
2 t Splenda® or 2 T Brown Sugar Blend Splenda®
1 t baking powder

1. Mix all the dry ingredients in a bowl.
2. Add the eggs and any additions and whisk until smooth. Add extract.
3. Spray a mini muffin pan with cooking spray and divide batter into 12 muffins.
Bake in a preheated oven at 350 degrees for 15-18 minutes.

Makes 12 mini muffins

ORANGE VANILLA MUFFINS
BASIC FLOURLESS OAT BRAN MUFFIN RECIPE

1 t orange extract
5 T fat free Orange yogurt
12 chocolate chips

GINGERBREAD MUFFINS
BASIC FLOURLESS OAT BRAN MUFFIN RECIPE

2 t DaVinci Gourmet™ Sugar free Gingerbread syrup
2 T fat free yogurt or 4 T canned pumpkin
1/4 t ground ginger
1 t cinnamon
1/4 t nutmeg
1/4 t ground cloves

APPLE CINNAMON MUFFINS
BASIC FLOURLESS OAT BRAN MUFFIN RECIPE
1 t vanilla
5 T fat free apple turnover yogurt
1 t cinnamon

CHOCOLATE PUMPKIN MUFFINS
BASIC FLOURLESS OAT BRAN MUFFIN RECIPE

1 t vanilla
4 T canned pumpkin
2 t unsweetened cocoa powder

Whole Wheat Oat Bran Cookies

BASIC WHOLE WHEAT OAT BRAN COOKIES

1/2 cup agave nectar
1/2 cup (1 stick) butter, room temperature
1 large egg
1/2 t vanilla extract
3/4-1 cup whole wheat pastry flour
1 t baking soda
1/4 t salt
1/4 cup oat bran

1. Beat the agave, butter and/or peanut butter, egg and vanilla by hand or in an electric mixer until creamy and fluffy.
2. Sift together the flour, soda, and salt, and blend it thoroughly with the oat bran and creamed mixture.
3. Fold any of the additions into the batter. Drop tablespoon-sized cookies on a sheet covered with parchment paper.
4. Bake at 350 for about 8-10 minutes.

Makes 1 1/2 dozen

PEANUT BUTTER MILK CHOCOLATE CHIP COOKIES
BASIC WHOLE WHEAT OAT BRAN COOKIE RECIPE
Replace stick of butter with 1/2 stick and 1/2 cup peanut butter
1/2 cup milk chocolate chips

OATMEAL RAISIN WHOLE WHEAT COOKIES
BASIC WHOLE WHEAT OAT BRAN COOKIE RECIPE
1 1/2 cups rolled oats
1/2 t cinnamon
1/2 cup raisins

CHERRY CHOCOLATE WHOLE WHEAT COOKIES
BASIC WHOLE WHEAT OAT BRAN COOKIE RECIPE
1/2 cup semi-sweet chocolate chips
1/2 cup dried sour cherries

66

Oats and Fruit Breakfast Bars

BASIC OATS AND FRUIT BREAKFAST BARS

1 1/2 cups quick oats
1/2 cup whole wheat flour
1/2 cup oat bran
1/2 t baking soda
1/2 t salt
1 t cinnamon
2 T Brown Sugar Blend Splenda® or 2 t Splenda®
1 egg
4 T butter, melted
1/4 cup canola oil
2 T fat free plain Greek yogurt

1. Line a square brownie pan with parchment paper and coat with cooking spray.
2. Mix all the wet ingredients together in one bowl and all the dry in another. Combine them and mix well.
3. Spread the oat mixture on the bottom of the dish, saving a few tablespoons for the top, and follow with the fruit filling. Sprinkle the oats on top and bake at 350 for 30 minutes.

Makes 16 2-inch bars

PEANUT BUTTER AND APPLE BREAKFAST BARS
BASIC OATS AND FRUIT BREAKFAST BARS RECIPE

1/2 cup natural peanut butter
4 apples, peeled, cored and cut into 1/2-inch thick slices
1/2 t cinnamon
2 T agave syrup or 2 t Splenda®
1 t cornstarch mixed with 1 T water

1. Replace the butter and oil with the peanut butter.
2. In a saucepan, combine apples, cinnamon and sweetener and cook for about 5 minutes.
3. Add cornstarch mixture.
4. Cook until the fruit thickens, about 1 more minute.

RASPBERRY COCOA BREAKFAST BARS
BASIC OATS AND FRUIT BREAKFAST BARS RECIPE

2 T unsweetened cocoa-added to the dry ingredients
4 oz fresh raspberries, slightly crushed
2 T agave syrup or 2 t Splenda®
1 t cornstarch mixed with 1 T water

1. In a saucepan, combine raspberries and sweetener and cook for about 5 minutes.
2. Add cornstarch mixture.
3. Cook until the fruit thickens, about 1 more minute.

Oats and Fruit Breakfast Bars

OATMEAL PLUM BREAKFAST BARS
BASIC OATS AND FRUIT BREAKFAST BARS RECIPE
4 plums, halved and cut into 1/2-inch thick slices
2 T agave syrup or 2 t Splenda®
1 t cornstarch mixed with 1 T water

1. In a saucepan, combine plums and sweetener and cook for about 5 minutes.
2. Add cornstarch mixture.
3. Cook until the fruit thickens, about 1 more minute.

Peanut Butter Granola Bars

ALISHA'S BASIC PEANUT BUTTER GRANOLA BARS

1/2 cup honey
1/2 cup natural peanut butter (I drain off any excess oil that is sitting on the top)
2 cups quick oats
1/2 cup flaxseed meal
1/2 cup oat bran

Instructions:
1. Heat the honey and peanut butter on low heat until combined. Remove from heat and let it cool.
2. Pour honey mixture over oats and additional ingredients from options below and mix well with hands.
3. Press onto a sheet covered with parchment paper and either let set overnight or refrigerate for about an hour. Cut into 2-inch squares. Store in an airtight container.

Makes 16 2-inch bars

CHERRY CHOCOLATE GRANOLA BARS
BASIC PEANUT BUTTER GRANOLA BAR RECIPE
1/4 cup sunflower seeds
1/2 cup peanuts
1/2 cup dried tart cherries
1 oz dark chocolate, roughly chopped
1 oz dark chocolate, melted

See-Instructions. Add all the nuts and cherries. After it cools even a bit more, add the chocolate chunks.

ALMOND RAISIN GRANOLA BARS
BASIC PEANUT BUTTER GRANOLA BAR RECIPE
1/2 cup almonds, roughly chopped
1/2 cup raisins
1/2 cup peanuts

See-Instructions. Add all the nuts and raisins.

CASHEW BANANA GRANOLA BARS
BASIC PEANUT BUTTER GRANOLA BAR RECIPE
1/2 cup cashews
1/2 cup dried banana chips, roughly broken
1/2 cup peanuts

See-Instructions. Add all the nuts and bananas.

Index

Index

Special Order Recipes

DukanItOut.com by **Special Order Recipes** is the website I started with Nicole Thomson when we began following the Dukan Diet. It is full of many recipes similar to what you will find in this book.

SpecialOrderRecipes.com is the new website we started that focuses on healthy living and delicious recipes. I use whole foods, whole grains and substitute natural sweeteners when possible. Special Order's concept of adapting recipes to fit one's lifestyle and tastes is my goal.

Contact: Janice@specialorderrecipes.com

Recipes Inspired By:
Dr. Pierre Dukan   http://dukandiet.com

For more Dukan Diet-inspired recipes check out:

UK Dukan Recipe website: http://mydukandiet.com/
Run by Joanna Goodshef, Author of "Delicious Dieting: The Oat Bran Guide" available on Amazon.com, featuring recipes from DukanItOut.com

CPSIA information can be obtained
at www.ICGtesting.com
Printed in the USA
270836LV00002B